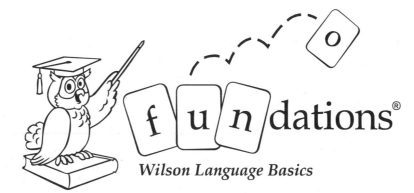

Wilson Language Basics

Composition Book

Level 1

SECOND EDITION

Wilson Language Training Corporation

www.wilsonlanguage.com

www.fundations.com

Fundations® Composition Book 1

Item # F2STCBK1

ISBN 978-1-56778-506-7

SECOND EDITION

PUBLISHED BY:

Wilson Language Training Corporation
47 Old Webster Road
Oxford, MA 01540
United States of America

(800) 899-8454

www.wilsonlanguage.com

Printed in the U.S.A.

November 2019

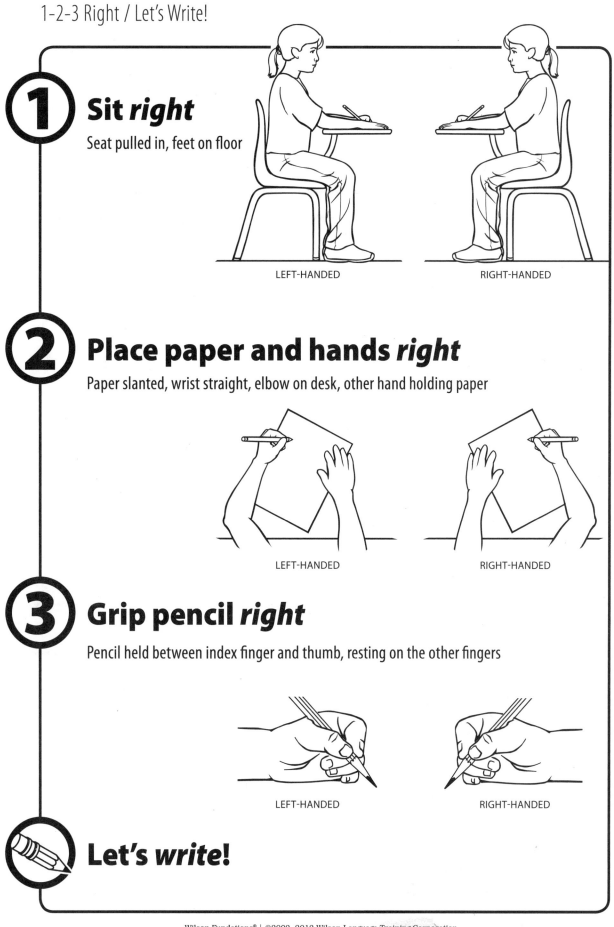

1 **Sit** *right*

Seat pulled in, feet on floor

LEFT-HANDED   RIGHT-HANDED

2 **Place paper and hands** *right*

Paper slanted, wrist straight, elbow on desk, other hand holding paper

LEFT-HANDED   RIGHT-HANDED

3 **Grip pencil** *right*

Pencil held between index finger and thumb, resting on the other fingers

LEFT-HANDED   RIGHT-HANDED

Let's *write!*

Sounds

1   2   3

Review Words

1   2

Current Words

1   2

Trick Words

1   2

Sentence

1

Sounds

1   2   3

Review Words

1   2

Current Words

1   2

Trick Words

1   2

Sentence

1

Sounds

1   2   3

Review Words

1   2

Current Words

1   2

Trick Words

1   2

Sentence

1

Sounds

1   2   3

Review Words

1   2

Current Words

1   2

Trick Words

1   2

Sentence

1

Sounds

1   2   3

Review Words

1   2

Current Words

1   2

Trick Words

1   2

Sentence

1

Sounds

1   2   3

Review Words

1   2

Current Words

1   2

Trick Words

1   2

Sentence

1

Sounds

1 _____ 2 _____ 3 _____

Review Words

1 _____ 2 _____

Current Words

1 _____ 2 _____

Trick Words

1 _____ 2 _____

Sentence

1 _____

Sounds

_____

- -

1 _____ 2 _____ 3 _____

_____

Review Words

_____

- -

1 _____ 2 _____

_____

Current Words

_____

- -

1 _____ 2 _____

_____

Trick Words

_____

- -

1 _____ 2 _____

_____

Sentence

_____

- -

1 _____

_____

_____

- -

_____

_____

Sounds

1   2   3

Review Words

1   2

Current Words

1   2

Trick Words

1   2

Sentence

1

Sounds

1   2   3

Review Words

1   2

Current Words

1   2

Trick Words

1   2

Sentence

1

Sounds

1   2   3

Review Words

1   2

Current Words

1   2

Trick Words

1   2

Sentence

1

Sounds

1 _____ 2 _____ 3 _____

Review Words

1 _____ 2 _____

Current Words

1 _____ 2 _____

Trick Words

1 _____ 2 _____

Sentence

1 _____

Sounds

1   2   3

Review Words

1   2

Current Words

1   2

Trick Words

1   2

Sentence

1

Sounds

1   **2**   **3**

Review Words

1   **2**

Current Words

1   **2**

Trick Words

1   **2**

Sentence

1

Today's Date: _____ *Check-up* ☐

Sounds

1   2   3

Review Words

1   2

Current Words

1   2

Trick Words

1   2

Sentence

1

Wilson Fundations® | ©2002, 2012 Wilson Language Training Corporation

Sounds

1   2   3

Review Words

1   2

Current Words

1   2

Trick Words

1   2

Sentence

1

Sounds

_____

- -

1   2   3

_____

Review Words

_____

- -

1   2

_____

Current Words

_____

- -

1   2

_____

Trick Words

_____

- -

1   2

_____

Sentence

_____

- -

1

_____

_____

- -

_____

_____

Sounds

1   2   3

Review Words

1   2

Current Words

1   2

Trick Words

1   2

Sentence

1

Sounds

_____

- -

1 _____ 2 _____ 3 _____

_____

Review Words

_____

- -

1 _____ 2 _____

_____

Current Words

_____

- -

1 _____ 2 _____

_____

Trick Words

_____

- -

1 _____ 2 _____

_____

Sentence

_____

- -

1 _____

_____

_____

- -

_____

_____

Sounds

1   2   3

Review Words

1   2

Current Words

1   2

Trick Words

1   2

Sentence

1

Sounds

1   2   3

Review Words

1   2

Current Words

1   2

Trick Words

1   2

Sentence

1

Sounds

1   2   3

Review Words

1   2

Current Words

1   2

Trick Words

1   2

Sentence

1

Sounds

_____

- -

1 _____ 2 _____ 3 _____

_____

Review Words

_____

- -

1 _____ 2 _____

_____

Current Words

_____

- -

1 _____ 2 _____

_____

Trick Words

_____

- -

1 _____ 2 _____

_____

Sentence

_____

- -

1 _____

_____

_____

- -

_____

_____

Sounds

_____

- -

1 _____ 2 _____ 3 _____

_____

Review Words

_____

- -

1 _____ 2 _____

_____

Current Words

_____

- -

1 _____ 2 _____

_____

Trick Words

_____

- -

1 _____ 2 _____

_____

Sentence

_____

- -

1 _____

_____

_____

- -

_____

_____

Sounds

1 I   all 2 for 3 off

Review Words

1 we do 2 and like

Current Words

1 now mo make 2 are

Trick Words

1 he to go 2 is

Sentence

1 the my you

me look help

Sounds

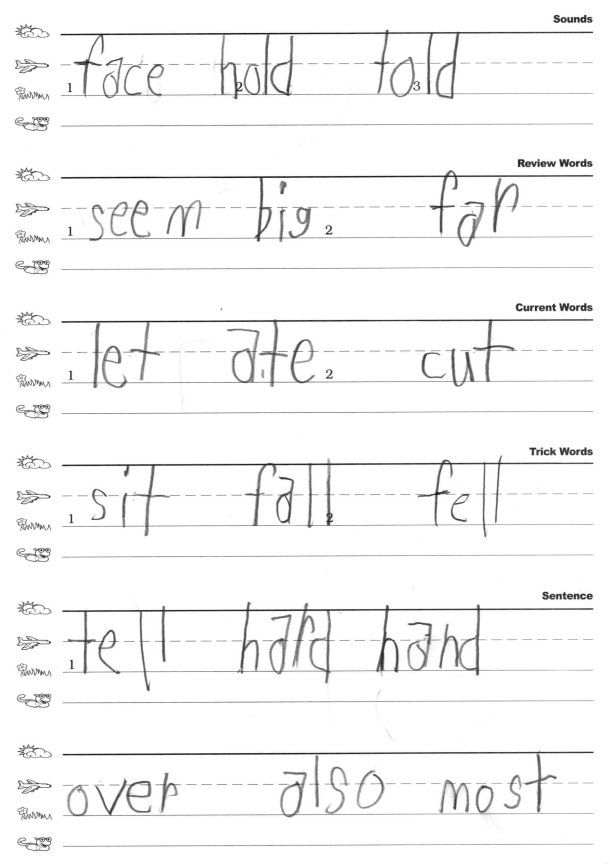

1 face 2 hold 3 told

Review Words

1 seem big 2 far

Current Words

1 let ate 2 cut

Trick Words

1 sit fall 2 fell

Sentence

1 fell hard hand

over also most

Sounds

1 _____ 2 _____ 3 _____

Review Words

1 _____ 2 _____

Current Words

1 _____ 2 _____

Trick Words

1 _____ 2 _____

Sentence

1 _____

Sounds

1 _____ 2 _____ 3 _____

Review Words

1 _____ 2 _____

Current Words

1 _____ 2 _____

Trick Words

1 _____ 2 _____

Sentence

1 _____

Sounds

_____

- -

1 _____ 2 _____ 3 _____

_____

Review Words

_____

- -

1 _____ 2 _____

_____

Current Words

_____

- -

1 _____ 2 _____

_____

Trick Words

_____

- -

1 _____ 2 _____

_____

Sentence

_____

- -

1 _____

_____

_____

- -

_____

_____

Sounds

1 _____ 2 _____ 3 _____

Review Words

1 _____ 2 _____

Current Words

1 _____ 2 _____

Trick Words

1 _____ 2 _____

Sentence

1 _____

Sounds

1   2   3

Review Words

1   2

Current Words

1   2

Trick Words

1   2

Sentence

1

Sounds

1   2   3

Review Words

1   2

Current Words

1   2

Trick Words

1   2

Sentence

1

Sounds

1 _____ 2 _____ 3 _____

Review Words

1 _____ 2 _____

Current Words

1 _____ 2 _____

Trick Words

1 _____ 2 _____

Sentence

1 _____

Sounds

1   2   3

Review Words

1   2

Current Words

1   2

Trick Words

1   2

Sentence

1

Sounds

1   2   3

Review Words

1   2

Current Words

1   2

Trick Words

1   2

Sentence

1

Sounds

1 _____ 2 _____ 3 _____

Review Words

1 _____ 2 _____

Current Words

1 _____ 2 _____

Trick Words

1 _____ 2 _____

Sentence

1

Sounds

Review Words

1 _____   2 _____

Current Words

1 _____   2 _____

Trick Words

1 _____   2 _____

Sentence

1 _____

Wilson Fundations® | ©2002, 2012 Wilson Language Training Corporation

Sounds

1   2   3

Review Words

1   2

Current Words

1   2

Trick Words

1   2

Sentence

1

Sounds

1 _____ 2 _____ 3 _____

Review Words

1 _____ 2 _____

Current Words

1 _____ 2 _____

Trick Words

1 _____ 2 _____

Sentence

1 _____

Sounds

1   2   3

Review Words

1   2

Current Words

1   2

Trick Words

1   2

Sentence

1

Sounds

1   2   3

Review Words

1   2

Current Words

1   2

Trick Words

1   2

Sentence

1

Sounds

1   **2**   **3**

Review Words

1   **2**

Current Words

1   **2**

Trick Words

1   **2**

Sentence

1

Sounds

1 _____ 2 _____ 3 _____

Review Words

1 _____ 2 _____

Current Words

1 _____ 2 _____

Trick Words

1 _____ 2 _____

Sentence

1 _____

Check-up ☐

Sounds

1 _____ 2 _____ 3 _____

Review Words

1 _____ 2 _____

Current Words

1 _____ 2 _____

Trick Words

1 _____ 2 _____

Sentence

1 _____

Sounds

1   2   3

Review Words

1   2

Current Words

1   2

Trick Words

1   2

Sentence

1

Sounds

1   2   3

Review Words

1   2

Current Words

1   2

Trick Words

1   2

Sentence

1

Sounds

1 _____ 2 _____ 3 _____

Review Words

1 _____ 2 _____

Current Words

1 _____ 2 _____

Trick Words

1 _____ 2 _____

Sentence

1 _____

Sounds

_____

- -

1   2   3 _____

_____

Review Words

_____

- -

1   2 _____

_____

Current Words

_____

- -

1   2 _____

_____

Trick Words

_____

- -

1   2 _____

_____

Sentence

_____

- -

1 _____

_____

_____

- -

_____

_____

Sounds

1   2   3

Review Words

1   2

Current Words

1   2

Trick Words

1   2

Sentence

1

Sounds

1 _____ 2 _____ 3 _____

Review Words

1 _____ 2 _____

Current Words

1 _____ 2 _____

Trick Words

1 _____ 2 _____

Sentence

1 _____

Sounds

1   2   3

Review Words

1   2

Current Words

1   2

Trick Words

1   2

Sentence

1

Sounds

1   2   3

Review Words

1   2

Current Words

1   2

Trick Words

1   2

Sentence

1

Sounds

1 _____ **2** _____ **3** _____

Review Words

1 _____ **2** _____

Current Words

1 _____ **2** _____

Trick Words

1 _____ **2** _____

Sentence

1 _____

Sounds

_____

- -

1 _____ 2 _____ 3 _____

_____

Review Words

_____

- -

1 _____ 2 _____

_____

Current Words

_____

- -

1 _____ 2 _____

_____

Trick Words

_____

- -

1 _____ 2 _____

_____

Sentence

_____

- -

1 _____

_____

_____

- -

_____

_____

Sounds

_____

- -

1 _____ 2 _____ 3 _____

_____

Review Words

_____

- -

1 _____ 2 _____

_____

Current Words

_____

- -

1 _____ 2 _____

_____

Trick Words

_____

- -

1 _____ 2 _____

_____

Sentence

_____

- -

1 _____

_____

_____

- -

_____

_____

Sounds

1   2   3

Review Words

1   2

Current Words

1   2

Trick Words

1   2

Sentence

1

Sounds

_____

- -

1 _____ 2 _____ 3 _____

_____

Review Words

_____

- -

1 _____ 2 _____

_____

Current Words

_____

- -

1 _____ 2 _____

_____

Trick Words

_____

- -

1 _____ 2 _____

_____

Sentence

_____

- -

1 _____

_____

_____

- -

_____

_____

Sounds

1 _____ 2 _____ 3 _____

Review Words

1 _____ 2 _____

Current Words

1 _____ 2 _____

Trick Words

1 _____ 2 _____

Sentence

1 _____

Sounds

_____

– –

1 _____ 2 _____ 3 _____

_____

Review Words

_____

– –

1 _____ 2 _____

_____

Current Words

_____

– –

1 _____ 2 _____

_____

Trick Words

_____

– –

1 _____ 2 _____

_____

Sentence

_____

– –

1 _____

_____

_____

– –

_____

_____

Sounds

1   2   3

Review Words

1   2

Current Words

1   2

Trick Words

1   2

Sentence

1

Sounds

1   2   3

Review Words

1   2

Current Words

1   2

Trick Words

1   2

Sentence

1

Today's Date: _____ _Check-up_ ☐

Sounds

1   2   3

Review Words

1   2

Current Words

1   2

Trick Words

1   2

Sentence

1

Wilson Fundations® | ©2002, 2012 Wilson Language Training Corporation   **63**

Sounds

1   2   3

Review Words

1   2

Current Words

1   2

Trick Words

1   2

Sentence

1

Check-up ☐

Sounds

_____

- -

1 _____ 2 _____ 3 _____

_____

Review Words

_____

- -

1 _____ 2 _____

_____

Current Words

_____

- -

1 _____ 2 _____

_____

Trick Words

_____

- -

1 _____ 2 _____

_____

Sentence

_____

- -

1 _____

_____

_____

- -

_____

_____

Sounds

1   2   3

Review Words

1   2

Current Words

1   2

Trick Words

1   2

Sentence

1

Sounds

1 _____ 2 _____ 3 _____

Review Words

1 _____ 2 _____

Current Words

1 _____ 2 _____

Trick Words

1 _____ 2 _____

Sentence

1 _____

Sounds

1 _____ 2 _____ 3 _____

Review Words

1 _____ 2 _____

Current Words

1 _____ 2 _____

Trick Words

1 _____ 2 _____

Sentence

1 _____

Today's Date: _____ *Check-up* ☐

Sounds

1 _____ 2 _____ 3 _____

Review Words

1 _____ 2 _____

Current Words

1 _____ 2 _____

Trick Words

1 _____ 2 _____

Sentence

1 _____

Sounds

1   2   3

Review Words

1   2

Current Words

1   2

Trick Words

1   2

Sentence

1

Sounds

1   2   3

Review Words

1   2

Current Words

1   2

Trick Words

1   2

Sentence

1

Sounds

_____

- -

1 _____ 2 _____ 3 _____

_____

Review Words

_____

- -

1 _____ 2 _____

_____

Current Words

_____

- -

1 _____ 2 _____

_____

Trick Words

_____

- -

1 _____ 2 _____

_____

Sentence

_____

- -

1 _____

_____

_____

- -

_____

_____

Sounds

Review Words

1 _____   2 _____

Current Words

1 _____   2 _____

Trick Words

1 _____   2 _____

Sentence

1 _____

Sounds

1   2   3

Review Words

1   2

Current Words

1   2

Trick Words

1   2

Sentence

1

Sounds

1   2   3

Review Words

1   2

Current Words

1   2

Trick Words

1   2

Sentence

1

Letter Formation

a

Wilson Fundations® | ©2002, 2012 Wilson Language Training Corporation

Sounds

1 _____   2 _____

3 _____   4 _____

5 _____   6 _____

7 _____   8 _____

9 _____   10 _____

Unit Test Grading			
Letter Formation:	_____ / 25	x 4	= _____ / 100
Sounds:	_____ / 10	x 10	= _____ / 100

Sounds

1 e   2 d   3 t

4 B   5 x

Words

1 d   u g   n a 2 p

3 z d   9   n a 4 d

5 b e g   F o 6 x

7 r e t   r o 8 b

quit

Wilson Fundations® | ©2002, 2012 Wilson Language Training Corporation

Words

9 h i t   m a d   10

Sentences

1 _____

2 _____

Unit Test Grading				
Sounds: **5** / 5	Words: **1** / 10	Score: _____		
Sentences: _____			x 4	
Words: _____ / 5	Trick Words: _____ / 5	Total Score: _____ / 100		
☐ Legibility	☐ Capitalization	☐ Punctuation	☐ Phrasing	

Sounds

1 H   M 2

3 P   O 4

5

Words

1 Hot   dah 2

3 maF   HoK 4

5 hEK

Sentences

1 _____

_____

2 _____

_____

Unit Test Grading			
Sounds: _____ / 5	Sentences:		Score: _____
Words: _____ / 5	Words: _____ / 5		x 4
Marking: _____ / 5	Trick Words: _____ / 5	Total Score: _____ / 100	

☐ Legibility ☐ Capitalization ☐ Punctuation ☐ Phrasing

Sounds

1   2

3   4

5

Words

1   2

3   4

5

Sentences

1 _____

2 _____

Unit Test Grading

Sounds: _____ / 5	Sentences:		Score: _____
Words: _____ / 5	Words: _____ / 5		x 4
Marking: _____ / 5	Trick Words: _____ / 5	Total Score: _____ / 100	

☐ Legibility ☐ Capitalization ☐ Punctuation ☐ Phrasing

Sounds

1   2

3   4

5

Words

1   2

3   4

5

Sentences

1 _____

2 _____

Unit Test Grading			
Sounds: _____ / 5	Sentences:	Score: _____	
Words: _____ / 5	Words: _____ / 5	x 4	
Marking: _____ / 5	Trick Words: _____ / 5	Total Score: _____ / 100	
☐ Legibility	☐ Capitalization	☐ Punctuation	☐ Phrasing

Sounds

1   2

3   4

5

Words

1   2

3   4

5

Sentences

1 _____

2 _____

Unit Test Grading

Sounds:	____ / 5	Sentences:		Score:	____
Words:	____ / 5	Words:	____ / 5		x 4
Marking:	____ / 5	Trick Words:	____ / 5	Total Score:	____ / 100

☐ Legibility   ☐ Capitalization   ☐ Punctuation   ☐ Phrasing

Sounds

1   2

3   4

5

Words

1   2

3   4

5

Wilson Fundations® | ©2002, 2012 Wilson Language Training Corporation

Sentences

1 _____

2 _____

Unit Test Grading

Sounds: _____ / 5	Sentences:	Score: _____	
Words: _____ / 5	Words: _____ / 5	x 4	
Marking: _____ / 5	Trick Words: _____ / 5	Total Score: _____ / 100	

☐ Legibility ☐ Capitalization ☐ Punctuation ☐ Phrasing

Sounds

_____

- -

1 _____ 2 _____

_____

_____

- -

3 _____ 4 _____

_____

_____

- -

5 _____

_____

Words

_____

- -

1 _____ 2 _____

_____

_____

- -

3 _____ 4 _____

_____

_____

- -

5 _____

_____

Sentences

1 _____

2 _____

Unit Test Grading

Sounds: _____ / 5	Sentences:	Score: _____	
Words: _____ / 5	Words: _____ / 5	x 4	
Marking: _____ / 5	Trick Words: _____ / 5	Total Score: _____ / 100	

☐ Legibility   ☐ Capitalization   ☐ Punctuation   ☐ Phrasing

Sounds

1 _____   2 _____

3 _____   4 _____

5 _____

Words

1 _____   2 _____

3 _____   4 _____

5 _____

Sentences

1 _____

2 _____

_____

Unit Test Grading

Sounds: _____ / 5	Sentences:		Score: _____	
Words: _____ / 5	Words: _____ / 5		x 4	
Marking: _____ / 5	Trick Words: _____ / 5	Total Score: _____ / 100		

☐ Legibility ☐ Capitalization ☐ Punctuation ☐ Phrasing

Sounds

_____

- -

1 _____   2 _____

_____

_____

- -

3 _____   4 _____

_____

_____

- -

5 _____

_____

Words

_____

- -

1 _____   2 _____

_____

_____

- -

3 _____   4 _____

_____

_____

- -

5 _____

_____

Sentences

1

2

Unit Test Grading

Sounds: _____ / 5	Sentences:		Score: _____		
Words: _____ / 5	Words: _____ / 5		x 4		
Marking: _____ / 5	Trick Words: _____ / 5		Total Score: _____ / 100		

☐ Legibility   ☐ Capitalization   ☐ Punctuation   ☐ Phrasing

Sounds

1 _____   2 _____

3 _____   4 _____

5 _____

Words

1 _____   2 _____

3 _____   4 _____

5 _____

Sentences

1

2

Unit Test Grading

Sounds: _____ / 5	Sentences:		Score: _____	
Words: _____ / 5	Words: _____ / 5		x 4	
Marking: _____ / 5	Trick Words: _____ / 5		Total Score: _____ / 100	

☐ Legibility   ☐ Capitalization   ☐ Punctuation   ☐ Phrasing

Sounds

1   2

3   4

5

Words

1   2

3   4

5

Sentences

1 _____

2 _____

Unit Test Grading			
Sounds: _____ / 5	Sentences:		Score: _____
Words: _____ / 5	Words: _____ / 5		x 4
Marking: _____ / 5	Trick Words: _____ / 5		Total Score: _____ / 100
☐ Legibility	☐ Capitalization	☐ Punctuation	☐ Phrasing

Sounds

1   2

3   4

5

Words

1   2

3   4

5

Sentences

1

2

Unit Test Grading

Sounds: _____ / 5	Sentences:		Score: _____	
Words: _____ / 5	Words: _____ / 5		x 4	
Marking: _____ / 5	Trick Words: _____ / 5		Total Score: _____ / 100	

☐ Legibility   ☐ Capitalization   ☐ Punctuation   ☐ Phrasing

Sounds

_____

- -

1 _____ 2 _____

_____

_____

- -

3 _____ 4 _____

_____

_____

- -

5 _____

_____

Words

_____

- -

1 _____ 2 _____

_____

_____

- -

3 _____ 4 _____

_____

_____

- -

5 _____

_____

Sentences

1

2

Unit Test Grading

Sounds: _____ / 5	Sentences:	Score: _____
Words: _____ / 5	Words: _____ / 5	x 4
Marking: _____ / 5	Trick Words: _____ / 5	Total Score: _____ / 100

☐ Legibility   ☐ Capitalization   ☐ Punctuation   ☐ Phrasing

Sounds

1 _____ 2 _____

3 _____ 4 _____

5 _____

Words

1 _____ 2 _____

3 _____ 4 _____

5 _____

Sentences

1 _____

2 _____

Unit Test Grading

Sounds: _____ / 5	Sentences:	Score: _____	
Words: _____ / 5	Words: _____ / 5	x 4	
Marking: _____ / 5	Trick Words: _____ / 5	Total Score: _____ / 100	

☐ Legibility   ☐ Capitalization   ☐ Punctuation   ☐ Phrasing

Sounds

1 _____ 2 _____

3 _____ 4 _____

5 _____

Words

1 _____ 2 _____

3 _____ 4 _____

5 _____

Sentences

1 _____

2 _____

Unit Test Grading

Sounds: _____ / 5	Sentences:	**Score:** _____
Words: _____ / 5	Words: _____ / 5	x 4
Marking: _____ / 5	Trick Words: _____ / 5	Total Score: _____ / 100

☐ Legibility   ☐ Capitalization   ☐ Punctuation   ☐ Phrasing

NOTES

Capitalization and Punctuation

Capital Letters

A B C D E F
G H I J K L
M N O P Q R S
T U V W X Y Z

Capitalization

- Beginning of sentence: <u>T</u>he dog is cute.
- People's names: <u>J</u>ohn and <u>M</u>aria are here.
- Specific names of places: <u>L</u>ong <u>P</u>ond, <u>W</u>isconsin
- Days of the week, months of the year: <u>F</u>riday, <u>J</u>une
- Beginning word in quote: Mr. Smith said, "<u>Y</u>es, I will go!"

Punctuation

- Period (**.**): I am six years old.
- Question Mark (**?**): When will you visit?
- Exclamation Point (**!**): I love this class!

Other:
- Comma (**,**): September 1, 2012
- Quotes (**" "**): She asked, "How are you?"

Mark My Words

Underline digraph

s<u>h</u>op   ba<u>th</u>   du<u>ck</u>

Star the bonus letters

ba<u>ll</u>⭐   pu<u>ff</u>⭐   fi<u>ll</u>⭐   ki<u>ss</u>⭐

Box the welded sounds

b⸤all⸥   h⸤am⸥   f⸤an⸥   r⸤ing⸥   p⸤ink⸥

Underline baseword, circle suffix

<u>bug</u>ⓢ   <u>hill</u>ⓢ   <u>can</u>ⓢ

Underline each sound in a blend

<u>f</u><u>l</u>ash   <u>s</u><u>t</u>ump   <u>s</u><u>c</u>rap

Mark closed syllable

<u>căt</u>   <u>ĕlf</u>
c   c

Mark vowel-consonant-e syllable

<u>bāke̸</u>   <u>stōne̸</u>
v-e   v-e